# PRAIRIE DOGS

Meryl Magby

PowerKiDS press.

New York

Published in 2012 by The Rosen Publishing Group, Inc.
29 East 21st Street, New York, NY 10010

First Edition

Editor: Amelie von Zumbusch
Book Design: Ashley Drago

Photo Credits: Cover, pp. 6, 7 (left, right), 20, 21 (bottom), 22 Shutterstock.com; pp. 4–5 © www. iStockphoto.com/Nicholas Homrich; pp. 8, 12–13 Raymond K. Gehman/Getty Images; p. 9 Jeff Foott/Getty Images; p. 10 © www.iStockphoto.com/Brad Sauter; pp. 11, 14 iStockphoto/Thinkstock; p. 15 (left) © www.iStockphoto.com/David Parsons; p. 15 (right) © www.iStockphoto.com/Orchidpoet; p. 16 Gail Shumway/Getty Images; p. 17 Wendy Shattil and Bob Rozinski/Getty Images; p. 18 Eastcott Momatiuk/Getty Images; p. 19 Martyn Colbeck/Getty Images; p. 21 (top) © www.iStockphoto.com/ John Henderson.

Library of Congress Cataloging-in-Publication Data

Magby, Meryl.
  Prairie dogs / by Meryl Magby. — 1st ed.
      p. cm. — (American animals)
  Includes index.
  ISBN 978-1-4488-6182-8 (library binding) — ISBN 978-1-4488-6323-5 (pbk.) —
ISBN 978-1-4488-6324-2 (6-pack)
  1. Prairie dogs—Juvenile literature. I. Title.
  QL737.R68M3314 2012
  599.36'7—dc23

                                              2011027917

Manufactured in the United States of America

CPSIA Compliance Information: Batch #WW12PK: For Further Information contact Rosen Publishing, New York, New York at 1-800-237-9932

# Contents

# Tunnel Builders

When Europeans first arrived in North America, billions of small animals called prairie dogs lived in underground tunnels across the Great Plains. Prairie dogs also lived in the deserts and mountains of western North America. Today, prairie dogs still live in these areas. Their **population** is much smaller, though.

Prairie dogs are great diggers. They build long systems of tunnels in which to live. These prairie dogs are sitting at a tunnel opening.

French traders called these animals *petits chiens*, which means "little dogs" in French. Prairie dogs are not really dogs, though. They are a kind of **rodent** called a ground squirrel. Prairie dogs are closely related to tree squirrels, chipmunks, and marmots. The only place in the world prairie dogs live is North America.

# Built to Dig!

Prairie dogs are small, furry animals with short tails. Their strong legs and long toenails make it easy for them to dig holes in the ground. Many prairie dogs have light brown fur. This helps them blend in with the dirt where they live. They weigh between 1 and 3 pounds (.5–1.4 kg).

There are five **species**, or kinds, of prairie dogs. These are the Utah prairie dog, the

A prairie dog's eyes are set far apart on each side of its head. This lets it see a wide area at one time.

Prairie dogs have five toes on each foot.

Black-tailed prairie dogs are most often between 14 and 17 inches (36–43 cm) long.

white-tailed prairie dog, the black-tailed prairie dog, the Gunnison's prairie dog, and the Mexican prairie dog. Black-tailed prairie dogs are the most common kind of prairie dog in the United States.

# Deserts, Valleys, and Grasslands

Utah prairie dogs live the farthest west of any kind of prairie dog. This Utah prairie dog is in Utah's Bryce Canyon National Park.

In the United States, prairie dogs can be found in many parts of the West. Gunnison's prairie dogs are found along the borders of New Mexico, Colorado, Arizona, and Utah. The white-tailed prairie dog lives in Colorado, Utah, Wyoming, and Montana. Utah prairie dogs live only in the mountain valleys of central Utah.

Black-tailed prairie dogs can be found all over Great Plains states east of the Rocky Mountains.

Different species of prairie dogs live in different **habitats**. Gunnison's prairie dogs, white-tailed prairie dogs, and Utah prairie dogs live in high deserts and mountain valleys. Black-tailed prairie dogs live in low, dry grassland areas.

The prairie dogs that live on the Great Plains are black-tailed prairie dogs.

# Burrows and Colonies

This prairie dog is keeping watch for predators.

Prairie dogs build their own homes. These homes are called burrows. Burrows are deep tunnel-like holes in the ground. Many burrows make up a prairie dog **colony**, or town. The burrows in a colony are connected to each other by lots of underground tunnels. The tunnels make it easy for prairie dogs to get away from **predators**.

This picture shows part of a prairie dog colony. How many burrow entrances can you count?

Prairie dogs build their colonies in places where there is no tall grass growing. This is because prairie dogs like to be able to see predators from a long way away. Large piles, or mounds, of dirt surround the entrances to their burrows. These mounds keep the burrows from flooding when it rains.

# Prairie Dog Facts

1. Prairie dogs have very good eyesight and hearing. They often watch and listen for nearby predators from on top of the large dirt mounds in their colonies.

2. Prairie dogs in the same family greet each other by sniffing each other's mouths or touching their teeth. This looks like they are kissing each other!

**3.** Prairie dogs like to eat plants that have a lot of water in them. Many of these animals live in places where water can be hard to find.

**4.** Prairie dogs bark to let other prairie dogs know there is danger nearby. They have different-sounding barks for different kinds of threats. When they bark, they often stand up on their back legs and throw their front legs in the air.

**5.** If you ever see a prairie dog up close, do not feed it human food. Human food is hard for prairie dogs to eat. It could even kill them!

**6.** Prairie dog colonies can be huge. One colony of black-tailed prairie dogs in Texas covered 25,000 square miles (64,750 sq km)!

**7.** Utah prairie dogs are the smallest prairie dogs. Black-tailed prairie dogs are the biggest prairie dog species.

# Life in the Coterie

These prairie dogs are greeting each other by touching their mouths together.

Prairie dogs live together in families, called **coteries**. A coterie is generally made up of an adult male prairie dog, several adult female prairie dogs, and their babies. Each coterie has a **territory** of about 1 acre (.4 ha).

Coteries are very close families. The prairie dogs in a coterie spend time digging burrows, **grooming** each other, and playing together. The adult male in the coterie is in charge of keeping their territory safe. Prairie dogs bark to warn each other if predators or prairie dogs from other families are nearby. Prairie dog barks sound much squeakier than dog barks.

The prairie dogs in one coterie often live in between 50 and 60 connected burrows.

This prairie dog is barking to warn others that there is a predator nearby.

# A Litter of Pups

Mother prairie dogs take good care of their babies. They will fight to keep their babies safe if they are in danger.

Adult prairie dogs generally **mate** in March or early April. About a month after they mate, female prairie dogs have a **litter** of between one and six babies. The babies are called pups. They are born blind and hairless. They stay with their mothers in their burrows for about six weeks to grow strong. Then, they explore the outside world.

At first, prairie dog pups drink their mothers' milk. However, they start looking for their own food after they are old enough to leave the burrow. Most prairie dogs live for about five to seven years.

# Finding Food

Grasses are the main food for black-tailed prairie dogs, such as this one.

Prairie dogs eat mostly plants, such as **forbs**, flowers, seeds, grasses, and leaves. Some prairie dogs also eat insects.

Prairie dogs are active only during the daytime. This is when they look for food. Throughout the year, prairie dogs store extra fat in their bodies. This helps them get through the fall and winter months when there is not a lot of food for them to eat. Prairie dogs that live in high mountain areas **hibernate**, or spend most of the winter in a sleep-like state. In fact, the black-tailed prairie dog is the only kind of prairie dog that does not hibernate.

This black-tailed prairie dog is looking around on a snowy winter day in South Dakota's Badlands. Black-tailed prairie dogs are active all winter long.

# Prairie Dogs in Danger

Though prairie dogs have many predators, their good eyesight and warning system can make them hard to catch.

Prairie dogs are important to many of the animals that share their habitats. Predators such as badgers, coyotes, foxes, bobcats, golden eagles, hawks, and black-footed ferrets depend on prairie dogs for food. Rabbits, weasels, snakes, burrowing owls, and other animals make their homes in old prairie dog burrows.

If prairie dogs die out, the animals that share their habitats and depend on them could die out, too. To keep all of these animals safe, people need to make sure that prairie dogs are doing well. We can try to keep these animals from getting sick. We can see that people do not poison or hunt them, too.

Coyotes are one of many animals that hunt prairie dogs. Like prairie dogs, these members of the dog family live only in North America.

American badgers live in western North America. They are good at digging. They often hunt prairie dogs by digging them out of their underground homes.

# Prairie Dogs Today

Prairie dog populations have gotten much smaller since Europeans first arrived in North America. In fact, the Utah prairie dog is considered a **threatened species** by the US government. This means that the government is worried that the species might be in danger of dying out.

However, many government **agencies** and wildlife groups are working to make sure that prairie dogs do not die out. There are many places you can see prairie dogs in the United States today, including national parks.

Prairie dogs live in several national parks, such as North Dakota's Theodore Roosevelt National Park and South Dakota's Wind Cave National Park.

# Glossary

agencies (AY-jen-seez)  Special departments of the government.

colony (KAH-luh-nee)  A place where a group of animals live together.

coteries (KOH-teh-reez)  Prairie dog families.

forbs (FORBZ)  Kinds of herbs that are not grasses.

grooming (GROOM-ing)  Cleaning the body and making it appear neat.

habitats (HA-buh-tats)  The kinds of land where an animal or a plant naturally lives.

hibernate (HY-bur-nayt)  To spend the winter in a sleep-like state.

litter (LIH-ter)  A group of animals born to the same mother at the same time.

mate (MAYT)  To come together to make babies.

population (pop-yoo-LAY-shun)  A group of animals or people living in the same place.

predators (PREH-duh-terz)  Animals that kill other animals for food.

rodent (ROH-dent)  An animal with gnawing teeth, such as a mouse.

species (SPEE-sheez)  One kind of living thing. All people are one species.

territory (TER-uh-tor-ee)  Land or space that animals guard for their use.

threatened species (THREH-tend SPEE-sheez)  An animal that is likely to become in danger of dying out.

# Index

# Web Sites

Due to the changing nature of Internet links, PowerKids Press has developed an online list of Web sites related to the subject of this book. This site is updated regularly. Please use this link to access the list:
www.powerkidslinks.com/aman/dogs/